Trumspringa

Natalie Dick

Presentation by *BookLeaf Publishing*

Web: www.bookleafpub.com

E-mail: info@bookleafpub.com

ISBN: 9789358316148

First edition 2023

Rain

I hate the rain
But it's always been there
though it only brings me pain
Rain seems to be the only one to care
I hate the rain
but everytime it pours
It washes away the stains
It washes my tears off shore
I hate the rain
But the rain does not hate me

Sadness

I'm afraid to be happy
afraid to leave my own sadness
I'm too comfortable in my unhappy
It's always been something I can turn to
Like a cold blanket that manages to keep me
warm
My sadness is not something new
It's something that makes me feel safe
I couldn't imagine leaving my sadness
It has become another face
My sadness is my favorite comfort
And definitely my favorite place

Room Tour

I'm not obsessed with my room
It's obsessed with me
Offering a place to hide
My room holds me so
Quietly my walls scream out
Grabbing me they cry
Telling me to stay inside

My floors cry
when I try to leave
How'd they die
if I didn't stay
But they lie

I'm not obsessed with my room
It's obsessed with me
The way my bed holds me so
I never want to leave
My room would never harm me
So believe me that
I'm not obsessed with my room

Scars of words

A string of words
pull in my stomach
Crawl up my throat
and twist in my mouth
They claw and scratch
trying to get out

My lips are sown
Always staying closed
Never breaking
Always staying still
But they tangle

How they wish to flee
If only they could
But my words stay still
Clumped together
Filling my stomach
Scaring my throat

Melody

You say our spark was too bright
that I only let you burn
but I held you so tight
That your stomach would turn

I loved you too much
You felt suffocated by me
You only saw me as a crutch
I saw you as the sea

I needed you to live
You needed me to let go
Waiting for something to give
I waited for your love to grow

You were a song to me
But I was only your melody

Shadows

Alone with my thoughts
Their shadows growing closer
A serie of traughts
Never getting older

A blanket of darkness
Surrounds my eyes
I don't feel any farness
Only a closeness that ties

They follow my every move
Their steps never falter
Always looking smooth
My counciuness grows softer

Alone in my thoughts
Only a reverie that haunts

Empty House

I went in with you by my side
But i left alone
We were holding hands
but now yours is stone

Mine holds yours things
that you left behind
I open the door to an empty house
the air seems stale like it knew you were gone

The floors cry with every step
Screaming what i couldn't
It was too quiet without you

I sat on our bed fiddling with sheets
tears strolled down my face
Dear elise tell what it's like up there
Is there a hand to hold

The Fallen soldier

His body lies in my arms
I can feel him grow cold
In the distance I hear warning alarms
I hug him to me as if he were gold

Please don't leave me, my love
My legs have given out and I can't carry you
anymore
Please don't go to the above
I can't bear to think your smiles will be
nevermore

His body is broken
His breathing has stopped
God must have spoken
I stared at his face as my heart dropped

I hate this war
Can we please go back to before

All I can do

All I can do
is not to cry
Withered on a moon
Nowhere to fly

Humming this sad tune
Wondering why
You left me so soon
Without saying goodbye

Now all I do is cry
Alone in my room
And I cant lie
You've moved on I assume

I don't want to die
But I don't want to cry

Hourglass

As time kisses you I weap
there's no irony in your death
you just took a sudden leap
I try but I don't feel your breath

You don't wait to say goodbye
I find you incredibly cruel
You told me not to cry
But I break that unspoken rule

I can't go on without you
My time is running out
This hourglass is askew
Without you there's only doubt

This sand keeps falling
And I can't keep going

Love

Love is like a vine
it slowly creeps around you
Slowly stealing your time
It's feels scary but that's not true

When those flowers bloom
oh it's so beautiful
Don't be afraid of it's doom
Let it hold you, be wistful

Small Things

All the small things you do
Remind me why I love you
I love the way your lip twitches into a smirk
I love the way you love your work
I love the way you get excited about a new book
When you find something interesting I love the
way you look
I love the way your eyes light up
But I can tell you already have a full cup
I love all the small things you do
But they remind me that you don't love me too

Self Care

I'm picking my bones up
Shoving them under my skin
Sewing my limbs on
Piece by piece
Building myself back up
I'm not ashamed of this process
Everyone needs to heal
I'm not ashamed of a little self care

Time

Time is not my enemy
It is a wonderful gift
Watching the seasons change
The flowers grow
Loved ones get old
It's a wistful feeling
To know we are moved by time

Words

You say my words are not art
Instead of a rose
You received thorny insults
Those words were my heart
My love suffocated you
For your heart was too small to accept the
amount I had
I love my words
They are rays of light
Sculptures and masterpieces
But my words are not for everyone

Self Love

I apply bandages to my wounds
Kiss away the pain
And gently wash off the stains
My hands are scarred but they are not rough
I have been there for me since day one
I am so in love with me

Love of Another

Like my father loves my mother,
I want to love someone
Give myself wholly to another,
Feel the warmth of the one

Like a bee who loves a flower
I want someone to hold
Like fresh laundry from the dryer
I don't want to be cold

Like a field that loves a shower
I want to hold someone
I want to fully love another
Feel the love from the one

Like my father loves my mother
I want the love of another

A Lonely Flower

A beautiful flower sat alone on a hill
Animals loved the kind flowers smell laughing
and enjoying her chaotic energy like she was a
happy pill
The flower was happy but still it sat alone on a
hill
The animals would ask her for advice and she
would always give them her optimistic thoughts
And the loyal flower never asked for anything in
return even though she was distraught
As the loyal flower was slowly wilting she still
never asked anything, no water, no sun, no soil
she never asked for it even though none of it was
a lot
The silly flower sat alone on a hill
The hill, though some would think it meant
nothing it was a tall pile of her pain
The animals walked all over the hill, laughing
and enjoying the flowers wonderful smell
The silly flower would smile with them but
when they left she cried like the rain
Flowers smell the best when their dying and the
most beautiful smiles are the ones lying
No one ever saw the flower cry like the rain

No one ever saw how they we're walking on her
pain
So the flower sat on her hill alone but still she
would smile until
Someone would see that see was lying, that she
was crying that she was dying
And they would take her from that hill and put
her on their windowsill
Where they would give water, sun, soil and most
of all the love she so deserved

Halfway to You

I move halfway across the world
You're smile still there
I didn't leave you any word
I know it wasn't fair
But I couldn't say goodbye
I couldn't see those tears
I couldn't listen to you cry
So i sit with my fears
Halfway across the world
Missing your smile
And wishing you were here
And i wasn't there

A Blue Painting

How I love the colors of you
I love all of your imperfections
Oh how I love your blue
I love all of your complexions
I could stare at you for days
A world without you is unbearable
I wish you could see the ways
You make me feel so remarkable
How I love the colors of you
I hate how no one else sees
All your different shades of blue
I love how much you reflect the sea
Oh how I love all your hues
How I love the colors of you

Rain

Rain falling down
Hitting the roof
It makes me want to call you
You always loved the rain
But I had hated it
It made me insane
I'm slowly loving the rain
As you adore it I want to too
I'm sorry I hated it once
Now I kinda like the cloudy days it brings

www.ingramcontent.com/pod-product-compliance
Lightning Source LLC
LaVergne TN
LVHW050308200726
843509LV00015B/3227